C000000552

and the Trossachs
National Park

Compiled by
Hugh Taylor and Moira McCrossan

JARROLD
publishing

Mapping
sourced from | Ordnance Survey®

Acknowledgements

Kieron MacKenzie, DB Outdoor Systems, Kendal and Deuter Rucksacks for technical assistance and support, Ian Gardner, National Trust for Scotland.

Text:	Hugh Taylor and Moira McCrossan
Photography:	Hugh Taylor and Moira McCrossan
Editorial:	Ark Creative, Norwich
Design:	Ark Creative, Norwich

© Jarrold Publishing 2005

Jarrold Publishing
ISBN 0-7117-3860-2

While every care has been taken to ensure the accuracy of the route directions, the publishers cannot accept responsibility for errors or omissions, or for changes in details given. The countryside is not static: hedges and fences can be removed, field boundaries can alter, footpaths can be rerouted and changes in ownership can result in the closure or diversion of some concessionary paths. Also, paths that are easy and pleasant for walking in fine conditions may become slippery, muddy and difficult in wet weather, while stepping stones across rivers and streams may become impassable.

If you find an inaccuracy in either the text or maps, please write to or e-mail Jarrold Publishing at the addresses below.

First published 2005
by Jarrold Publishing

Printed in Belgium
by Proost NV, Turnhout. 1/05

Jarrold Publishing
Pathfinder Guides, Whitefriars, Norwich NR3 1TR
email: info@totalwalking.co.uk
www.totalwalking.co.uk

Front cover: Waterfall at Queen Elizabeth Forest Park
Previous page: Forest road in Bonnie Strathyre

Contents

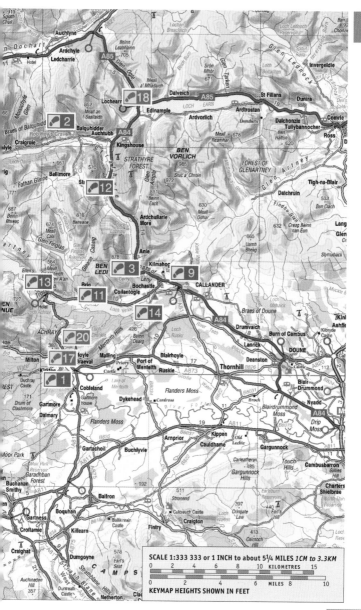

SCALE 1:333 333 or 1 INCH to about 5¼ MILES *1CM to 3.3KM*

0 2 4 6 8 10 KILOMETRES 15

0 2 4 6 MILES 8 10

KEYMAP HEIGHTS SHOWN IN FEET

Introduction

The walks in this book have been devised with families and children in mind. All of the walks have points of interest and a question designed to keep young minds occupied. Just over an hour from Edinburgh and less from Glasgow, Loch Lomond and the Trossachs is an area of contrasts, from the wild and remote glens of the Trossachs to the scenic beauty along the banks of Loch Lomond.

Loch Lomond and the Trossachs National Park

John Muir, a Scot from Dunbar, was the first person to call for action to preserve the wild places of the world. He was instrumental in founding the National Park Service in the USA and creating the modern ecology movement. Although he died in 1914, two years before the National Park Service was created, he is generally regarded as the father of the National Park. Americans have enjoyed access to thousands of square miles of National Park land for most of the 20th century.

Several National Parks have been created in England since the first one in the Peak District in 1951. In Scotland however it took a further 51 years of arguing and the establishment of a Scottish Parliament to create the country's first National Park, Loch Lomond and the Trossachs.

The military road to Inversnaid Garrison

Within the park are seven of the largest freshwater lochs in Scotland and a couple of seawater lochs, which reach in from the west coast as far as Arrochar. Countless smaller lochs and lochans lie between hills and glens, some of them linked by meandering rivers or rushing hill burns.

The area became a popular destination with those who

Balloch Castle

could afford to travel, following the publication of Sir Walter Scott's poem, *The Lady of the Lake* and his novel, *Rob Roy*, as readers sought out the locations in the book. The poet William Wordsworth along with his sister Dorothy and fellow poet Samuel Taylor Coleridge visited the area and undertook a couple of epic walks. Jules Verne inspired by his visit here wrote the novel *Les Indes noires* or *Black Diamonds*, situating a fictional coalmine under Loch Katrine. Felix Mendelssohn, the composer, got caught in a squall on Loch Lomond and almost drowned.

Queen Victoria's love of the Highlands and the arrival of the railway encouraged many more people from all classes of society to escape the city and enjoy the fresh air and spectacular open spaces of Loch Lomond and the Trossachs.

The landscape of the park was created about 450 million years ago by the intense heat and pressures that melted, pushed and distorted the underlying rocks. Later during the Ice Ages, huge glaciers slowly crossed the land gouging out the shape of the glens and lochs. Much later still human beings altered parts of this landscape by building settlements, roads and by agricultural improvements. This is where Lowland Scotland ends and Highland Scotland begins. The massive geological fault known as the 'Highland Line' or 'Highland Boundary Fault' runs across Loch Lomond and on through the Trossachs by way of Aberfoyle.

All of the walks in this book are inside the National Park. Many are on forest roads and are waymarked making them easy to follow even in winter. If you are not an experienced walker then start with the shorter ones at the front of the book. Even there you may find a few short but steep sections. The trick is to take it easy, slow down and walk at a pace that allows you to carry on a conversation without too much effort.

Famous footsteps

These walks are a grand introduction to Scotland's story. From ancient tracks and drove roads to military roads and railways, tread the ways used by the ancient Picts, the Roman Legions, Jacobite armies and Victorian travellers.

You can follow Rob Roy MacGregor across hillsides, where he lay in wait to pounce on unsuspecting cattle drovers or tramp the trails that he used while evading government forces. Visit his grave at Balquhidder then climb to a viewpoint above the village to look along the lochside route of his last journey.

Admire the views around Loch Venachar that inspired Sir Walter Scott's novels and enchanted Queen Victoria, then walk through a mountain pass in the footsteps of William and Dorothy Wordsworth. At Inversnaid walk along the remains of a military road and discover the ruins of an 18th-century garrison, now serving as a sheep pen behind a farmhouse.

Glen Croe from the 'Rest and Be Thankful'

Over in the west of the park look along Glen Croe and imagine the din and stir of ancient cattle droves, when a few hardy highlanders on foot herded hundreds of beasts down the glen to Balloch and onwards to the great cattle trysts of Crieff and Falkirk. Follow the old military road along the same glen and after the steep climb to the top realise why it is called the 'Rest and Be Thankful'.

Loch Long from Arrochar

Natural history

Throughout the park there is a great richness of natural history. You can see the majestic golden eagle soaring high above a mountain pass or a buzzard swoop on its prey over marshland. The fortunate will see otters, foxes and maybe even the shy pine martin but most will see red and roe deer and red squirrels. In the forests there are ancient Scots' pines that have stood for centuries, massive oaks, alder, birch and rowan as well as the ubiquitous Sitka spruce planted in regimented lines during the second half of last century. Many of those plantations have now reached maturity and are being harvested providing an opportunity to see again the landscape as it once was.

These walks are Scotland in microcosm. There is water everywhere reflecting the sky and the forests and the hillsides in still clear lochs or tumbling down crags and glens in rushing white torrents. There is the fresh smell of damp forests in the morning and wood smoke at night. The colour may be as bright as blue skies and fresh green meadows, or as rich as autumn gold all around and underfoot, or as dim as misty mountains wreathed in cloud.

1 *The fairies on Doon Hill*

START Aberfoyle Trossachs Discovery Centre (grid ref: NN 521009)
DISTANCE 2 miles (3.2km)
TIME 1½ hours
PARKING Free in Aberfoyle
ROUTE FEATURES Lanes; pavements; footpaths and woodland. Mainly flat but moderately steep climb to the hilltop

The Reverend Robert Kirk was minister of Aberfoyle. His daily routine included taking a stroll to the top of Doon Hill where he would talk to the fairies that lived there. This might seem strange today but not in the 17th century when most people still believed in magical little people.

Walk along the car park away from the Trossachs Discovery Centre. Turn left into Manse Road and cross a bridge **A**.

Continue along this road to reach Aberfoyle cemetery **B**. Go through the cemetery gate then veer right and cross to the ruins of the church. At the rear of the building you'll find the grave of the Reverend Kirk. According to local tradition he's not buried there and if the grave were to be opened it would be empty. Leave the cemetery by the gate opposite the church,

Children love seeing the offerings to the fairies

PUBLIC TRANSPORT Bus from Glasgow, Perth or Stirling
REFRESHMENTS The Forth Inn beside the car park
PUBLIC TOILETS At start
PICNIC/PLAY AREA Play area adjoining car park
ORDNANCE SURVEY MAPS Explorer 365 (The Trossachs)

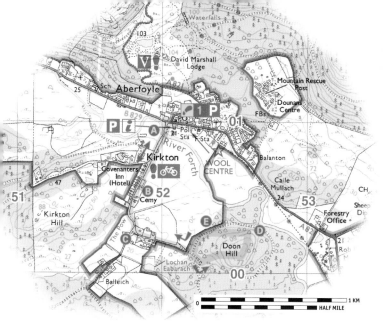

turn left and continue along the lane.

Where the road forks **C** just past Old Manse Gardens, go left and follow the red waymarked route for Doon Hill and Fairy Trail. Go

Most of the trees and bushes on the summit of Doon Hill have ribbons and coloured strips of cloth tied to their branches. These are offerings that people have left for the fairies and are supposed to bring **good luck**. Some have **messages** attached, most asking for help from the fairies. One is from someone wishing for a skateboard. You can leave something for the fairies too if you like. What will you wish for?

through a gate and keep an eye open for dog teams because this is also part of a husky training route. Pass a turning on your right then head steeply uphill to reach a red waymarker and a sign pointing to Doon Hill Fairy Trail.

Turn left onto a well-surfaced footpath and follow it uphill through the woods. Be very quiet and careful now as you do not want to do anything to upset the fairies. The Reverend Kirk spent much of his life studying the ways of the fairies – how they lived, what they ate, the homes they lived in and their fears, beliefs and superstitions.

? What are the two heavy iron coffin-shaped boxes by the door to the church?

Eventually he wrote a book about them called *The Secret Commonwealth of Elves, Fauns and Fairies*. It is still in print today and you can probably get a copy at the information centre at the car park.

Near the top of the hill the path divides. Turn right and take the narrower path to the summit and head towards the large tree in the centre. When the minister wrote his book in 1691 it made the fairies very angry because they did not want mortals to know about them. According to legend they captured him and spirited him away to the top of Doon Hill where he was imprisoned for eternity in the roots of this tree. Public records tell another story. They reveal that the minister died of a heart attack and was buried in his own churchyard. He suffered his heart attack on the summit of Doon Hill however, so there are local people who, to this day, still believe that the body buried in the churchyard was a changeling that the fairies substituted for the burial.

When you leave the summit take the third path marked by a red waymarker **D** and head downhill. At the foot of the hill turn left onto a track by a red waymarker **E**. After 109 yds (100 m) turn right at a T-junction back onto the lane and retrace your steps to the car park. ●

The ruined church and graveyard at Kirkton

Balquhidder and Rob Roy MacGregor

2

START Balquhidder church (grid ref: NN 536209)
DISTANCE 2 miles (3.2km)
TIME 1 hour
PARKING Limited free parking at church
ROUTE FEATURES Forest roads; footpaths; hillside and woodland

The character of Rob Roy, the highland outlaw, as portrayed in the novel by Sir Walter Scott and later in a motion picture by Liam Neeson is largely romantic, but the man who roamed this countryside in the 17th and early 18th century was a swashbuckling rogue, who paid scant regard to the laws of the land.

Walk from the car park along a lane that heads gently uphill to the right of the church. Cross a stile **A** and continue along a forest road through woodland following the green waymarkers and signposts pointing to Creag an Tuirc. After approximately ½ mile (800m) with the road rising gently you will come to a green building on the right **B**.

Turn right and keep going uphill on another forest road. This is Rob Roy country, where in the dense heather-clad hills the outlaw would hide whenever army forces were

after him. Born in 1671, the third son of Lieutenant Colonel Donald MacGregor of Glengyle, he was known as Rob Roy because of his red hair, (from the Gaelic for red). After his marriage he lived near Inversnaid, rented grazing land at Balquhidder and became a prosperous cattle dealer. Things went wrong when one of his men disappeared with money he had borrowed from the Marquis of Montrose. Montrose had him charged with embezzlement and when he failed to answer the summons, he was declared an outlaw and his family evicted from

PUBLIC TRANSPORT None
REFRESHMENTS The Library Tearoom
PUBLIC TOILETS None
ORDNANCE SURVEY MAPS Explorer 365 (The Trossachs)

The grave of Rob Roy MacGregor at Balquhidder

their home. Rob Roy was given a lease on land in Breadalbane but, as an outlaw, was unable to trade as a cattle dealer so he turned instead to an early protection racket from which the word 'blackmail' entered the English language. He travelled the country rustling cattle then demanding money to return them.

Pass a conveniently situated bench where you can stop for a short rest.

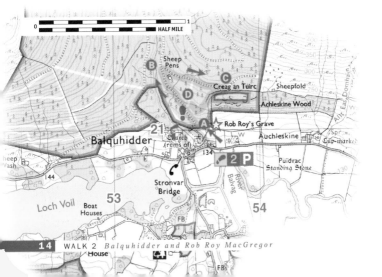

? *What is inscribed on Rob Roy's gravestone?*

Continue to a bend in the road opposite a gate **C**. Turn right through the gate then cross a burn. Head uphill on some stone steps and beyond them a path that goes through a stand of old Scots' pines to reach the summit of Creag an Tuirc. From the seat you will find here you can sit and enjoy some of the finest views in the Highlands. Look along the length of Loch Voil and the Braes of Balquhidder rising to the side of it. Along here, past the head of the loch and near the banks of the River Larig was the house of Inverlochlarig where Rob Roy spent the last years of his life. For a man who had lived most of his life by the sword his death was a peaceful one in his own bed on December 28, 1734. His funeral procession marched down the length of the glen on New Year's Day 1735 with a MacGregor piper leading the way. You'll find his grave in front of the ruined church beside the car park. Retrace your steps back downhill but take a left turn where the path forks. Follow this downhill, across some bridges and a stile eventually to reach the forest road **D**.

Turn left and follow this back to the stile behind the church. Turn right over the stile and walk along the path to cross a bridge. Continue on the footpath to reach the road opposite the Old Library Tearoom. Turn left and continue along the road to the car park. ●

The forest road to Creag an Tuirc

Throughout history there are accounts of wealthy men and women spending money to improve the lot of the common people. One of them, **David Carnegie**, of Stronvar Estate in Balquhidder was anxious to stop his workers spending much of their leisure time in the local ale house. He built a library opposite it and encouraged them to learn to read. The library is now a tearoom but the pub still sells beer.

3 *The Falls of Leny*

This short walk does not stray far from the road but there is a sense of peace and isolation as the historic path meanders through lovely woodland by the river right up to the falls. Although not dramatic in terms of height, the river cascades in foaming torrents around the rocks and boulders of the pass.

START Car park by the River Leny (grid ref: NN 587095)
DISTANCE 1½ miles (2.4km)
TIME 1 hour
PARKING Car park at start of walk
ROUTE FEATURES Surfaced cycle path; woodland footpath; riverside

The walk starts from a small car park on the far side of the River Leny from the A84 and is reached by taking the first left turning after Kilmahog then turning left onto a dirt road running beside the river.

Long ago, before the development of a road system in Scotland, the Pass of Leny was one of the most important routes in the country. Countless travellers used it to get from Lowland to Highland Scotland from the dawn of history. From the mysterious Picts and early Romans to marauding highlanders and cattle rustlers like Rob Roy, Jacobite soldiers and

On foot or bike this walk is very popular

army redcoats, they tramped this pass to hunt, to trade or go to war.

From the car park head south along the river. Go through a gate on the right and continue along the National Cycle Network route 7 then cross a tributary burn by a

PUBLIC TRANSPORT Bus from Callander
REFRESHMENTS None
PUBLIC TOILETS None
ORDNANCE SURVEY MAPS Explorer 365 (The Trossachs)

small bridge. Soon after you will pass the remains of an old railway bridge.

Early tourists, inspired by the novels of Sir Walter Scott, visited this famous beauty spot and from 1870 their numbers increased when the Callander to Oban Railway was opened. The railway continued to run until 1965 when a rock fall resulted in its closure. This was only a matter of weeks before the cuts proposed by Dr Beeching would have closed it anyway. The old railway track bed has since been resurfaced and is now the Lowland Highland trail part of the National Cycle Network route 7.

Turn left at a stone bench **Ⓐ**, leaving the cycle path and continuing, still parallel to the river, along a footpath through woodland. This walk is particularly beautiful in autumn, when the colours of the woodland are spectacular. Look out for another path below you on your left and take a left turn to reach it. Continue

In 1961 Dr Richard Beeching was appointed chairman of the British Railways Board by the Minister of Transport. He was charged with making the railways profitable and undertook a survey to determine which railway lines were losing money. He published his report *The Reshaping of British Railways* in 1963. It showed that half of the network was underused and uneconomic. The **'Beeching Plan'** finalised in 1965 recommended the closure of about 8000 miles of track and 2000 stations.

following this path along the river-bank to reach the falls.

Carry on the path past the falls then head uphill still going in the same direction as the river. When you come to a T-junction turn left. Soon after this look out for a crossroads, where you turn right and head away from the river back towards the cycle path, which is now in view at a T-junction by a bridge about 100 yds (91m) away **B**. When you reach it turn right back onto cycle route 7 and keep on it to return to the start. ●

> **?** The section of the River Leny running down from the falls is called the Garbh Uisge. What does this mean in English?

The Falls of Leny

Inversnaid Garrison

START Loch Arklet Waterworks (grid ref: NN 353094)

DISTANCE 1½ miles (2.4km)

TIME 1 hour

PARKING On grass verge just before waterworks

ROUTE FEATURES Military road; rough hillside; road and farm track

4

This land, once owned by Rob Roy MacGregor, now belongs to the RSPB. They have removed all the sheep and plan to replant native forest. This will help to save Scotland's dwindling population of black grouse as well as providing a habitat for red kites and securing the hunting ground of the golden eagle.

Cross the road from the gate at Loch Arklet Waterworks and cross the fence. Veer left and go slightly uphill heading towards a visible notch between two wooden poles **Ⓐ**. This is part of the military road constructed in Glen Arklet in the early 18th century – part of a general scheme of military roads planned and constructed by General George Wade in the aftermath of the 1715 Jacobite Uprising. The roads were meant to enable quick movement of government troops through otherwise rough country. This was to ensure that the Highlands could be kept

The remains of the military garrison

under military surveillance and prevent any further insurrection. A wire fence now has to be negotiated and then you will ford a small burn. Many walks in Scotland involve the crossing of fences. Some have barbed wire on

PUBLIC TRANSPORT None

REFRESHMENTS Inversnaid Hotel

PUBLIC TOILETS None

ORDNANCE SURVEY MAPS Explorer 364 (Loch Lomond North)

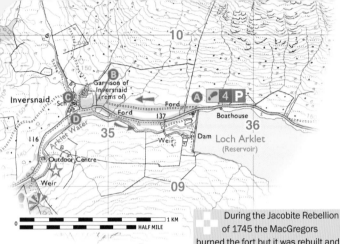

top and, while not essential, a useful piece of kit to carry is a length of old bicycle tyre. Slip this over the top strand of wire to avoid snagging clothing.

Keep following the same direction and once again the faint outline of the road will reappear. In wet weather this can be a very boggy walk and often you will have to negotiate sections by climbing on to the banks at the side. The effort is well worth it as the views are awesome.

Continue to cross another burn and make towards the white buildings of Garrison Farm. You may have to leave the line of the road occasionally to get round some of the boggier sections. Cross another burn and come to a fence,

where you have a choice. *You can climb this to continue on the road or turn right and head uphill a short distance to pass through a gate, then turn left to get back to the road.* Just before the next burn, turn left and follow a sheep track downhill. Go through a gate then cross the burn **B**. Turn right and head back uphill to pick up again the faint outline of the road and turn left along it. Now cross a fence, climb down a small banking and turn right onto a farm road **C**. Keep on it past the house then go through a gate.

At the rear of the farm steading the

Sheep pens where soldiers once slept

ruined buildings that are now part of a series of sheep pens are all that remains of Inversnaid Garrison. Return from here to the farm road, walk down it to the T-junction with the main road **D** and turn left. Continue along it to return to your car.

The **barracks** here were part of a series constructed in the early years of the 18th century. Ruthven near Kingussie is probably the most famous but it was **Inversnaid** which was completed first. They were built on land confiscated from Rob Roy MacGregor. Rob Roy did not give up his land quietly and resorted to kidnapping the workforce or warning them off on pain of death. Despite this the building was **completed by 1723**, two years before Ruthven.

? Who was the author who popularised the Highlands with his novel Rob Roy?

The clearly visible outline of Wade's road to Inversnaid

5 *Balmaha woodland trails*

START Balmaha Visitor Centre (grid ref: NS 420909)
DISTANCE 1¾ miles (2.8km)
TIME 1 hour
PARKING Free at visitor centre
ROUTE FEATURES Forest roads; paths

Balmaha is a sleepy little village on the east shores of Loch Lomond and has long been a popular destination for day-trippers and walkers. As well as this pleasant stroll along the banks of the loch and through the woodlands behind the car park, the area offers many more walking possibilities including the island of Inchcailloch.

Exit the car park onto the main road, cross it and turn right. Walk along the edge of the loch until you come to a waymarker by a gap in the wall **A**. Continue for a few yards to reach a wooden viewing platform.

Facing out to the loch you can see the group of islands along the line of the Highland Boundary Fault. Inchcailloch, Torrinch, Creinch and Inchmurrin. The Fault runs on behind you and through Conic Hill.

Return to the gap, cross the road to reach a footpath into the woods.

Inchcailloch Island can be reached by ferry from the boatyard at Balmaha where the ferry runs on demand. The island is a nature reserve renowned for its bird life. There are a variety of trails through the oak woods that cloak the island, the remains of the first parish church and a rather superb picnic site. It's open all year round but wardens are only present from May to September.

Continue along it to reach a waymarked junction at the rear of the visitor centre car park **B**. Keep straight ahead following blue waymarkers then pass to the right of a small pond. Continue uphill as

PUBLIC TRANSPORT Bus from Balloch
REFRESHMENTS Pub opposite car park
PUBLIC TOILETS In car park
ORDNANCE SURVEY MAPS Explorer 347 (Loch Lomond South)

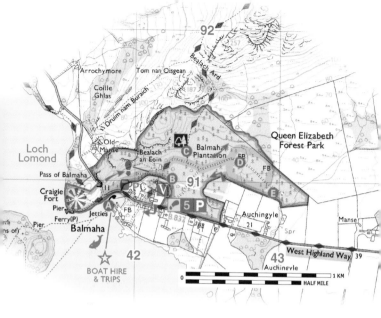

One of the well-surfaced footpaths in Balmaha Woods

the path climbs steadily. When you reach a junction to the left **C** keep straight ahead still following the blue waymarkers. *If you want to climb Conic Hill you would turn left here instead.* Follow the white thistle waymarks to reach the summit then return to this junction and continue on the blue route.

> **?** *What do the white thistle waymarks tell you about a path?*

At a T-junction with another path turn left, head uphill on a forest road and ignore the blue

Balmaha is a popular spot for boating on Loch Lomond

waymarked junction to your right. You will rejoin the path here on the return leg. Keep ahead for 100 yds (91m) then turn left onto a footpath opposite a solitary Scots pine **D** by a large boulder. You are now on a very pleasant woodland path that meanders through a section of Scots' pines. Soon the blue waymarkers will reappear to reassure you that you are on the right path. Continue through a clearing in the wood then enter another section of woodland and

continue until the path reaches a T-junction with the forest road **E**. Cross the road and continue into the woodland on the other side, again following the path marked by blue waymarkers.

Cross a couple of bridges and a small burn eventually to reach the T-junction at the forest road. Turn left here and retrace your route to the rear of the car park. Turn left into the car park and return to the car.   ●

The Tarbet Isle Loop

6

START A82 north of Tarbet (grid ref: NN 326053)
DISTANCE 1½ miles (2.4km)
TIME 1 hour
PARKING Car park just off road
ROUTE FEATURES Footpaths; woodland; hillside

This pleasant, waymarked, Forestry Commission path consists of a high road and a low road through woodland of Scots' pines, conifer and broad-leaved trees. There are some superb specimens of mature Scots' pines and oak trees and the remains of a section of the old military road that ran up Loch Lomond side to Crianlarich.

🖊 Head uphill from the car park on a forest road then turn left at a yellow waymarker **A** and continue on a well-surfaced footpath into the woods. Pause periodically to enjoy the views down the loch and across to the eastern side of Loch Lomond, where on a clear day Ben Lomond can be seen towering above everything else.

As the path continues through the wood it follows the line of a very old tumbledown wall covered in moss. When the wall turns right the path continues through a gap. Keep on this to reach a well-situated picnic table. This is a great

The well-surfaced footpaths make for easy walking

spot for an alfresco lunch, a short breather or just a stop to admire more breathtaking views. Just off

PUBLIC TRANSPORT Train from Glasgow
REFRESHMENTS Tarbet tearoom
PUBLIC TOILETS None
ORDNANCE SURVEY MAPS Explorer 364 (Loch Lomond North)

Tarbet or 'Tarbert' is derived from a Norse word for 'portage', a narrow strip of land where boats could be taken from the water and dragged overland to re-enter the water at the other end. This was how the longboats of the **Viking King Haakon** came from Loch Long to Loch Lomond to attack and pillage the communities there. Following the raid the Vikings were destroyed at the Battle of Largs in 1263.

the banks of the loch you will see Tarbet Isle. This is one of many islands on Loch Lomond and is privately owned.

Nearby, if you poke about a bit, you will find stretches of the old military road from

Tarbet to Crianlarich. This was a later phase of military road building – this time under the control of General Wade's successor, General Caulfield, in the years following the Battle of Culloden in 1746. Work started in 1752 and it was completed in 1754. Other sections of military road will be encountered elsewhere in the book where you will be able to walk along them. When you locate this section you'll soon see why it does not form part of the walk.

Looking over Tarbet Isle and Loch Lomond

Continue on the path from the picnic table and eventually it will snake down the hillside and follow the course of a burn. When you reach a junction **B**, near a car park, turn right and head back uphill passing some very old oak trees and a solitary rhododendron. As you continue to follow the yellow waymarkers the path will again wind downhill to pass through the remains of the wall a little downhill from where you crossed earlier. Through the trees you will catch glimpses of the outward section of the path. Continue until the path emerges from the trees near the start of the walk and the car park.

> **?** *Where is the military road?*

The variety of trees makes this an interesting walk in all seasons

7 *Balloch Castle Country Park*

START Balloch Castle Country Park (grid ref: NS 391831)
DISTANCE 2 miles (3.2km)
TIME 1 hour
PARKING Near the castle
ROUTE FEATURES Surfaced footpaths; easy gradients; suitable for pushchairs and wheelchairs

Glasgow Corporation bought Balloch Castle in the early 20th century and here created Loch Lomond Park. It soon became a favourite destination for Glasgow families who called it 'Glasgow's Garden'. The official name was changed to Balloch Country Park in 1980 and when the National Park was created in 2002 it was the only country park within its boundary.

Walk back along the road from the car park and turn right when you reach a crossroads Ⓐ. On your right is a magnificent old oak tree that's worth stopping to have a look at. Continue on this road to reach Balloch Castle.

Walking past the front of Balloch Castle

The present castle was built in 1808 by John Buchanan of Ardoch; a wealthy, local businessman who acquired the estate in 1790. He built his castle on the hill here overlooking the site of the old castle and it's easy to see why from the view you have over much of the parkland and across Loch Lomond. However Buchanan had a second reason for placing his new home here – it's visible for miles around and he wanted to impress people who were visiting the area! He inherited his wealth from his father who owned the largest

PUBLIC TRANSPORT Train or bus from Glasgow
REFRESHMENTS Tearoom in visitor centre
PUBLIC TOILETS In visitor centre
ORDNANCE SURVEY MAPS Explorer 347 (Loch Lomond South)

Buchanan designed the grounds surrounding the castle to resemble a **wild North American landscape**. Later owners added to his early work by planting the many monkey puzzle trees that you can now see and the rather ornate tulip trees. Over the years many of the shrubs have become overgrown obscuring some of the finer features of the landscape. A programme of extensive renovation that started in 2003 will have it restored to its former glory by 2006.

factory in Glasgow and who had also founded the Glasgow Ship Bank. When Buchanan became a partner he would often sign banknotes at his desk in the castle. Now the castle is a visitor centre where you can find out about the people who used to live and work here.

Walk round to the front of the castle and continue along the footpath **B**. When you reach a junction keep straight ahead. At the next junction turn left **C**. The path continues through woodland passing a collection of large beech trees then heads downhill and curves right to follow the banks of the loch. When you reach the next junction opposite a jetty keep straight ahead. From here you can see the large building of Loch Lomond Shores and the steamer *The Maid of the Loch*. Continue along the path until you are

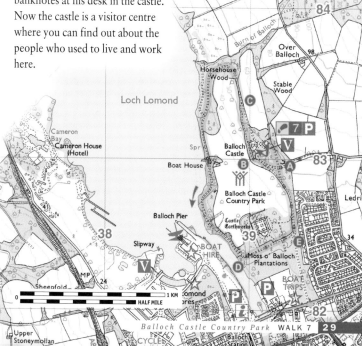

opposite the steamer jetty. On your left is the site of the original castle (NS 387825).

In the 13th century Balloch was the main crossing point on the River Leven where it flows from Loch Lomond. It was strategically important to the Earls of Lennox, who owned all the land in this area and built a castle to guard the entrance to the loch. They occupied it for 150 years before moving out to Inchmurrin. Some of the stones from the ruin of the old castle were later used in the construction of the present castle. All that remains of the original is a mound and an overgrown moat but if you look carefully you will be able to see the outline. The path forks at an interpretation board **D**. Go left.

Cross a bridge where the path bends left and continue along this through mature woodlands. Ignore all tracks turning off this road until you reach a T-junction **E**. Turn left here and continue along this road, climbing steadily to pass through the crossroads and return to the car park. ●

> **?** Ben Lomond comes from the Gaelic 'Beinn Laomainn' but what does this mean?

This walk heads down through parkland to the banks of Loch Lomond

The abandoned homestead of Sallochy Woods

START Sallochy Woods car park (grid ref: NS 380957)
DISTANCE 2 miles (3.2km)
TIME 1½ hours
PARKING Sallochy Woods car park
ROUTE FEATURES Forest path; loch side path; short rocky section

8

The woods here are part of the Queen Elizabeth Forest Park. This easy stroll through woodlands and by the loch side, takes in a ruined farm steading and lovely views of the loch. This eastern shore of the loch is much more peaceful than the busy western shore even in the height of summer.

Start at the car park and head towards the main road. At a signpost for the Sallochy Trail **A**, head to the right onto a track. Cross the road and continue along the trail, keeping the woodland on your right. Look out for the large oak trees as you walk round this trail. During the 18th and 19th centuries the woods were planted and harvested regularly for timber, but some of the best oak trees in each section were always left to grow on and there they remain in their ancient glory.

The ruins of Western Sallochy

? *What is the seed of an oak tree called?*

PUBLIC TRANSPORT None
REFRESHMENTS None
PUBLIC TOILETS None en route
ORDNANCE SURVEY MAPS Explorer 364 (Loch Lomond North)

Light-dappled paths and ferns in Sallochy Woods

When you come to a fork in the path **B**, take the right fork into the wood following the waymarker posts. Continue along the woodland path until you reach the ruined cottages at Western Sallochy **C**, the remains of a 19th-century farm.

They are a haunting sight in the clearing in the woods. Although life would have been hard for this isolated community, their ghosts seem to linger in this atmospheric little hamlet. Go right round the buildings to the left and follow the track to a T-junction at a waymarker **D**.

Turn right on to the forest road.

Follow the forest road for about ½ mile (800m) to a gate just before the junction with the main road **E**. Go over the gate and across the road and turn right. Then turn left onto a faint path **F**. Continue along towards the loch side to a well-surfaced footpath and turn right onto that **G**. This is the West Highland Way. Follow this waymarked path along the loch.

Loch Lomond is the largest area of fresh water in Britain. It is 24 miles (38km) long and five miles (8km) wide, with 38 islands that can be visited in summer from the boatyard just down the road at Balmaha. On the islands and

around the shores of the loch are havens for wildlife and an amazing 25% of all the plants that grow in the British Isles can be found here.

The path veers off on an uphill path through a rocky section and woodland over a knoll. There is some duckboarding laid over a boggy patch and the path eventually leads back to the car park. ●

At nearby Balloch there is a new visitor attraction, the **Loch Lomond Shores Gateway**. Within this, the **Drumkinnon Tower** has viewing galleries and shops, visitor information, interactive screens, theatre groups and musicians, as well as superb and informative audio visual shows on the big screen. It provides an excellent introduction to anyone wanting to explore the area.

Western Sallochy once a thriving small community

9 Callander to Kilmahog

START Riverside car park just off the A84 in Callander (grid ref: NN 625079)

DISTANCE 3 miles (4.8km)

TIME 1½ hours

PARKING Car park

ROUTE FEATURES Cycle path; footpaths; country lanes

This is a splendid low level walk through much of the history of the area. The walk is along a 21st-century cycle path built on the bed of a disused 19th-century railway. It passes the Iron Age fortifications of the earliest inhabitants, the ruined garrison of later Roman invaders and sites associated with early Christian missionaries.

From the car park turn right onto the cycle path by the riverside. Keep on the riverside path while passing a wooden walkway on your right. When you reach a T-junction turn left, then left again **Ⓐ**. At the next T-junction turn onto the cycle path to Strathyre. Next cross the river over a footbridge and continue on the cycle path.

Look out over the fields on your right to see the outline of the Roman fort (NN 614078). Bochastle Fort was an important northern outpost of the Roman

Woodland path on the Callander to Strathyre Cycle Route

PUBLIC TRANSPORT Bus from Stirling/Perth

REFRESHMENTS Cafés, pubs and restaurants in Callander

PUBLIC TOILETS Callander Tourist Information Centre

ORDNANCE SURVEY MAPS Explorer 365 (The Trossachs)

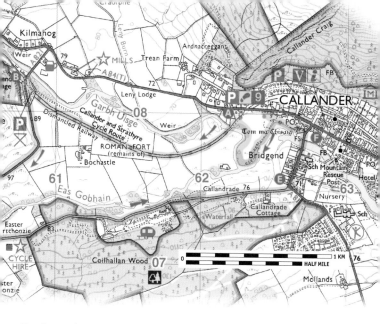

Empire. Built around AD85 during the governorship of Sallustius Lucullus it was occupied for a very short time. It was part of a series of forts known as the Glen Forts that were intended as a base from which to spearhead an advance into the Highlands. This came to nothing and Bochastle would have been abandoned no later than AD90 when the Romans pulled back south of the Forth and Clyde.

Cross a farm road then continue along the path to reach the car park at Kilmahog. Pass under a railway bridge beside Kilmahog car park and continue to reach a T-junction **B**. Kilmahog sits on the Highland Boundary Fault – a geological as well as cultural boundary between Lowland and Highland Scotland. The name comes from the Gaelic 'Cill mo Chug', meaning the Cell or Church of St Chug. Chug was a holy man who built his cell beside the River Leny by the Garbh Uisge, the Rough Water. Pilgrims made the journey to this cell and in time the early religious centre, which would become the settlement of Kilmahog built up round it.

Turn left onto the road. Pass the entrance to Bochastle car park on your right. *If you feel like a climb it's a short but strenuous hike from here to the summit* but the effort

This was once the Callander to Strathyre railway line

will be rewarded by a splendid view back along the old railway line and you'll get a better idea of the layout of the Roman fort. It is likely that a signal station existed here in Roman times to provide an early warning system of attackers

Callander is one of Scotland's earliest planned towns. It came about as a result of the **Jacobite Rebellion of 1745.** In an attempt to finally subdue the Highlands and prevent further outbreaks, the government embarked on building a network of military roads. They also planned to build towns along the roads hoping that clans' people would settle there making them easier to control.

approaching down the glens to the north or west.

Continue along the road to the next junction on the left signed for Invertrossachs **C**. On your right is Dunmore Fort. This Iron Age fort sits on the southern slopes of Ben Ledi. Dating from 700BC it has thick defensive walls and a commanding view along the valley.

> **?** *What does the name of the Iron Age Dunmore Fort mean?*

Turn left following the sign for Invertrossachs, cross a bridge to reach a T-junction **D** and turn left towards Callander. At the junction with the road to Callander Holiday Park keep left. Soon after reaching Callander there is a junction **E**. Turn left onto the A81. Follow this road to cross a bridge then turn right onto the cycle way **F** beside the river to return to the car park. The mound on your left as you approach the car park is 'Tom na Chessaig', the Hill of St Kessog. St Kessog was a follower of St Columba and like him came from Ireland. He gets the credit for having brought Christianity to this part of Scotland and it was on this hill that he preached in the 6th century. ●

Gartocharn and Loch Lomond Nature Reserve

10

START A811 Gartocharn
(grid ref: NS 428862)
DISTANCE 4 miles (6.4km)
TIME 2 hours
PARKING Lay-by on A811
opposite The Hungry
Monk
ROUTE FEATURES
Footpaths; fields;
woodland; loch side and
farm roads

The first part of this walk can be very boggy and heavy-going particularly in wet weather but it is well worth it for the wide variety of vegetation, and for the wildlife and birds that can be seen in the woods of the nature reserve and on the shores of the loch.

Turn right onto the road opposite The Hungry Monk pub **A**. Follow this road to the right passing a church and then the new community hall. At the far side of the hall turn left onto a rough footpath. Head downhill and go through a kissing-gate into a field. Walk along a rough and boggy footpath at the edge of the field beside a hedge. At the end of this field pass through a gap in the hedge and continue across a field.

Pass through a gap in the hedge at the end of the field and continue along the path. Follow it through a gap in some gorse bushes. From here the path continues and is surfaced with wooden sleepers. It is still however dreadfully muddy and hard going. When you reach a burn, turn right through a kissing-gate and follow the line of the burn. That's the worst of it past and the walking gets much easier from here.

When you reach another kissing-gate on your left, go through it and cross a bridge over the burn. This is a short but pleasant section of footpath which ends at a gate giving access to a lane. Turn right into the

PUBLIC TRANSPORT Bus from Balloch
REFRESHMENTS The Hungry Monk
PUBLIC TOILETS None
ORDNANCE SURVEY MAPS Explorer 347 (Loch Lomond South)

lane and proceed to its end at a T-junction opposite a white cottage **B**. Turn left then right at the next junction **C** following signs for Loch Lomond Nature Reserve. At the next junction keep left and continue along a rough road to reach the edge of the nature reserve. Go through two gates then follow the footpath through the woods.

Loch Lomond Nature Reserve includes five of the loch's islands. This section is part of a larger area of fen, grassland and swamp woodland round the mouth of the River Endrick. Depending on the time of year you are walking you will be able to see the tufted grasses and sedges that thrive here. Look out also for the Scottish dock which does not grow anywhere else in Britain. It loves the wet soil along the banks of the loch. There's another kissing-gate to go through then continue on the path. Late autumn, winter and early spring is a good time to visit because this is when the greylag

A dew-spangled spider's web

> **?** What is the name of the highest mountain on the east side of Loch Lomond?

Lots of interesting flora can be seen on this walk

and white-fronted geese can be seen. They arrive every year from Greenland and the sight of the huge skeins flying in over the loch is a joy to watch.

At the end of the woods you can continue along a rough track to reach some farmland. In the spring and summer the farmland in the reserve is a wildflower meadow. In the winter you may often find it flooded. At the end of the woods turn and retrace your steps to the junction with the white cottage. Keep ahead here and follow this country lane for a little over ½ mile (800m) to reach a junction for the road to Middle Gartocharn Farm **D**. Turn right and head uphill. Continue on the road, passing the farm steading then joining the road that passes the community hall. From here retrace your route to the start.

11 *Glen Finglas woodlands*

START Glen Finglas car park
(grid ref: NN 549062)
DISTANCE 4 miles (6.4km)
TIME 2 hours
PARKING Glen Finglas car park
ROUTE FEATURES Footpaths; roads; fields

Glen Finglas, the 'glen of white water', was traditionally a hunting estate used by the Scottish kings and nobility. It's one of Britain's largest surviving areas of upland wood pasture and the largest native broad-leaved forest belonging to Woodland Trust Scotland. This short walk is a brief introduction to what can be seen by those who would like to explore further.

Leave the car park on the footpath that heads towards the road. Keep on it passing the exit onto the road opposite Lendrick Lodge.

The path crosses a small burn then swings left and heads uphill. When you reach a waymarker at a junction **A**, turn right and follow the pink waymarks. The path climbs through woodland then goes through a kissing-gate to continue uphill to circle a rocky knoll. Climb the stone steps to the top of the knoll then stop for a breather and admire the view back downhill. This is particularly beautiful in autumn when the leaves are changing colour.

Continue from here along a well-trodden path through open countryside. In front of you, to the left, Ben Venue provides the perfect backdrop for Loch Achray while Glen Finglas opens out on your right. When you reach a waymarker on some large stones, turn right towards Glen Finglas.

Follow a rather boggy but well-waymarked section of path running alongside the mouldering

PUBLIC TRANSPORT Bus from Callander or Aberfoyle
REFRESHMENTS Brig o' Turk tearoom
PUBLIC TOILETS None
ORDNANCE SURVEY MAPS Explorer 365 (The Trossachs)

The footpath heads towards Ben Venue

remains of a stone wall. The path forks **B** near a white house on the road to your right. Take the left fork and soon join a farm track. Continue along it to reach a T-

> **?** *What does the name Brig o' Turk mean?*

junction with the road **C**, turn left onto a path just before the road and keep on it to arrive in the village of Brig o' Turk.

Walk through the village to the junction for The Byre Inn and the Duke's Pass **D**. Cross the road to the footpath opposite the junction and continue along it parallel to the road. When you reach the river **E** turn right onto the footpath that runs along the riverbank. Nearby is the Brig o' Turk. The last wild boars in Scotland were allegedly killed near here. Cross a road **F**, go through a kissing-gate and follow the path uphill through the woods. Look out for a charming rustic stool beside the kissing-gate that has been carved from an old tree stump. Leave the woodland and go through a

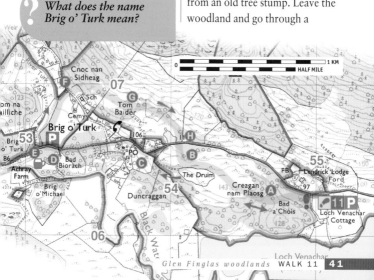

kissing-gate. Continue following the path through open countryside. At a junction **G** turn left to cross some duckboards and continue along a well-constructed stone footpath.

The path crosses some boggy ground on duckboards. To your right is the abandoned hut, which provided shelter when this boggy area served as the curling pond for the village. At a time in the past when winters in Scotland were much colder, many rural communities had a curling pond, where they would gather to enjoy the sport of curling. Milder winters coupled with the building of permanent ice rinks led to the decline of curling as an outdoor sport.

Exit the path via a kissing-gate **H**, cross the road to go through another kissing-gate and continue along the footpath. Head uphill towards a large boulder then keep left to reach a T-junction. Turn left here to rejoin the outward route then retrace your steps to the car park. ●

The path continues through woodland to Brig o' Turk

Bonnie Strathyre

12

START Forestry Commission car park at Strathyre (grid ref: NN 560168)
DISTANCE 4 miles (6.4km)
TIME 2 hours
PARKING Forestry Commission car park, Strathyre
ROUTE FEATURES Country roads and lanes; forest roads; footpaths; woodland; river

To enjoy the view on this walk there is a short but strenuous climb up a couple of footpaths. Both are well-surfaced and the climb is easy if taken at a slow pace. From the top you can see all the way up the glen to the former barracks on the military road that is now the Kingshouse Hotel.

At the rear of the car park, by the river, are the marker poles for the start of several walks. Head up a banking and turn right onto the footpath then cross a bridge and continue along the rear of some houses.

Strathyre was once a settlement on the opposite side of the river on the route of an old drove road. When the Callander to Oban Railway was constructed the village was moved to its present location.

After passing the village, go through a kissing-gate to turn left onto a road. Keep on this, crossing a bridge, then turning left when you reach a T-junction **A**. Immediately on the right there is a turning that you should take, then head uphill through the woods on a steep footpath.

The footpath terminates by a green and blue waymarker at a forest road. Turn right. Walk along the forest road keeping a sharp lookout for a narrow path heading uphill **B** to the left. Turn onto this and settle in for a long, slow climb through the trees. This path changes direction on several occasions but will eventually reach another forest road **C**. That's the

PUBLIC TRANSPORT Bus from Callander
REFRESHMENTS Hotels and tearoom, Strathyre
PUBLIC TOILETS None
ORDNANCE SURVEY MAPS Explorer 365 (The Trossachs)

hard part of the walk completed and it's fairly easygoing from here.

Turn right and stroll along the forest road. Soon you will leave the

> **?** *What kind of squirrel can you see in the forests here?*

tree cover and enjoy your first look at the magnificent view along Strathyre. William Wordsworth visited Strathyre in 1803 with his sister Dorothy and the poet Samuel Taylor Coleridge. They enjoyed walking in the hills and it was on one of these walks that the sight of a Highland lass working alone in a field up the glen inspired Wordsworth's poem, *The Solitary Reaper*. The road climbs gently at first then starts to descend. When you reach a junction beside a green waymarker **D** about two miles

> 'There's gold in them thar hills' or at least there once was. In the 19th century the second Marquis of Breadalbane, John Campbell, established a **gold mine** above the old railway station at **Balquhidder**. The Marquis was an amateur geologist and he was convinced that he could make a fortune extracting gold from the mountains on his estate. Although he found gold it was in such small amounts that it cost more to transport it than it was worth.

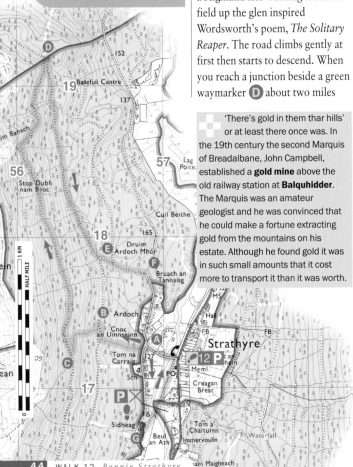

The long climb is rewarded by this view along Strathyre

(3.2km) into the walk, keep on the main road following it to the right, round a hairpin bend. You are now on the return leg.

The beauty of this glen was the inspiration for songwriter Sir Harold Boulton's piece that is most often associated with the area, *Bonnie Strathyre*:
'There's meadows in Lanark and mountains in Skye,
And pastures in Hielands and Lowlands forbye;
But there's nae greater luck that the heart could desire
Than to herd the fine cattle in bonnie Strathyre.'

Boulton was the writer of many popular songs that soon came to be regarded as traditional, probably because they were set to traditional tunes. His other famous works include *All Through The Night* and *The Skye Boat Song*.

At the next junction **E** turn left by a green waymarker, and head downhill. Go round a barrier at the bottom of the hill **F** and turn right onto a lane. Follow this into the village past the village school and several houses. Just past the last house **G** turn left opposite a Forestry Commission walks sign and take the footpath into the woods. Cross a burn by a footbridge then swing left to cross the river on a suspension bridge. From here it is a short distance back to the start of the walk and the car park . ●

13 Loch Katrine Dam and the Pass of the Trossachs

START Loch Achray Hotel (grid ref: NN 506063)
DISTANCE 3½ miles (5.6km)
TIME 2 hours
PARKING Lay-by on A821 near Loch Achray Hotel
ROUTE FEATURES Forest roads; woodland; loch side

The part of Scotland now known as the Trossachs is much larger than the narrow gorge between Loch Achray and Loch Katrine, which originally bore the name. Meaning the 'bristling country' it was at the heart of Clan MacGregor lands long before it became a Victorian tourist attraction and later the source of water for the city of Glasgow.

Walk along the road to the turn off for the Loch Achray Hotel **A**. Turn left and walk along the drive, then follow it as it skirts to the right of the hotel and then continues to the rear. Turn right here **B** to cross a bridge then continue along a forest road into the woods.

At a junction of forest roads **C** turn right. Ignore a turn off onto a footpath on the left and keep on the forest road. When the road ends cross a ladder-stile then continue along a boggy footpath passing a gate on your right.

The path gets much muddier as it heads uphill but will soon reach a ladder-stile on your right **D**. Cross this then turn right to head back downhill for a short distance. Now turn left to skirt the bottom of a knoll. The path is narrow here but keep on it heading uphill, then down a set of stone steps and through a gate to get onto the dam. *Take care crossing the dam particularly if you have children with you.* The views along Loch Katrine from here are breathtaking and this is a good place to take photographs. In the early morning

PUBLIC TRANSPORT Bus from Callander or Aberfoyle
REFRESHMENTS Queen Elizabeth Forest Park Visitor Centre
PUBLIC TOILETS None
ORDNANCE SURVEY MAPS Explorer 365 (The Trossachs)

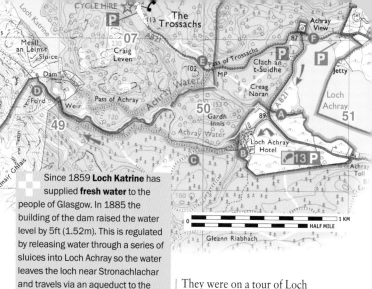

look out for the dew-hung spiders' webs on the fencing along the dam.

Once off the dam turn right onto a lane and continue along it. This is the Pass of Achray and as the lane moves away from the water's edge you will pass though some tranquil woodland. Eventually you will pass through a set of white gates to reach a T-junction with the A821 **E**. This is the Pass of the Trossachs and it was along here that the poet William Wordsworth, his sister Dorothy and their friend, the poet, Samuel Taylor Coleridge walked in 1803.

They were on a tour of Loch Lomond and had been ferried across from the west bank to Inversnaid. From there they walked along an old horse road to Loch Katrine where they debated whether to press on or return. From a passing horseman they learned of a gentleman's house round the head of the loch. This was probably Glengyle and there they managed to arrange accommodation for the night. In her journal, Dorothy wrote of the finely dressed lady of the house whose kitchen, by comparison, had a mud floor and walls. The next morning they continued along the side of the loch until they reached a ferryman's longhouse. There Wordsworth and his sister persuaded the ferryman to row

Boat house on the edge of Loch Katrine, by the dam

them to the south end of the loch but Coleridge preferred to walk. They met up with him when they got off the boat and following the ferryman walked through the Pass of the Trossachs, Dorothy delighting in the 'perfection of loveliness and beauty' of the surrounding hills, the heather, birch trees, rocks and knolls.

Turn right and walk along the road to the next junction **F**. From here you turn right again and follow the road round Loch Achray back to the start. The Wordsworths and Coleridge returned from here to the ferryman's rough dwelling where they spent the night. The next day they walked through driving rain, back round the head of the loch and from there back to Inversnaid. On the journey they met up with two young women, relatives of the Inversnaid ferryman. It was a Sunday and when they arrived in Inversnaid the ferry was across Loch Lomond taking people to church. The young women invited the party to wait in the cottage and dry their clothes by the fire. Shortly after his return from Scotland Wordsworth wrote his poem, *To the Highland Girl of Inversnaid*.

What is the name of the boat that sails on Loch Katrine during the summer months?

Loch Venachar and Invertrossachs

START East Lodge car park
(grid ref: NN 592055)
DISTANCE 4½ miles
(7.2km)
TIME 2½ hours
PARKING Forestry car park
just past East Lodge
ROUTE FEATURES
Woodland; forest roads
and lanes; spectacular
views

14

This is a walk of incredible beauty and majestic views. Starting with a gentle climb towards the Menteith Hills, the landscape at first gives no hint of what is to come. However, when you reach the point where the road overlooks the loch you will see what it was that inspired Sir Walter Scott and why Queen Victoria loved it.

Take the forest road heading uphill from the car park. The road climbs steadily at a very easy gradient. Ignore a junction on the right **A** and one on the left a bit farther on. There are a couple of pleasant waterfalls to pass on your left. They are at their best after spells of wet weather.

If you walk as quietly as you can and keep a good lookout you might see some of the varied wildlife that lives in this area. Red and roe deer are probably the most common and easily spotted. The tiny red squirrel still has a toe hold

here along with the reclusive pine martin, weasels, stoats and mink. Your patience may be rewarded by a view of one of these creatures foraging for food but more likely all you will get is a fleeting glance of something small with a whisking tail darting across a forest road.

> **?** *What are the decorations on the brightly painted millenium cycle path marker you'll pass on the walk?*

When you reach a junction **B** turn right and follow the path along the

PUBLIC TRANSPORT None
REFRESHMENTS None
PUBLIC TOILETS None
ORDNANCE SURVEY MAPS Explorer 365 (The Trossachs)

end of a lochan. Along the side of the lochan the road climbs uphill to pass a picnic table on top of a knoll on your right. All that is required to transform this little corner into paradise on earth is a spot of sunshine, a picnic and a bottle of dry white wine. Continue on the road heading uphill again then circle right past some crags to arrive at a junction **C**. Keep right here and stop in a few moments to enjoy the most spectacular views along Loch Venachar and across it to Ben Ledi rising above the northern shore.

The loch was formed during the last Ice Age by the huge sheets of ice that moved slowly over the land. These mile-thick sheets gouged out the shape of the lochs as they passed. It takes its name from the Gaelic 'bheanchair' which means 'horn-shaped' and refers to the tapered ends of the loch. These are no longer as prominent as they once were since the building of the dam at one end and subsequent rising of the water level. Follow this steep, winding road downhill to reach a T-junction onto a private road **D**.

On Thursday, September 2, 1869, **Queen Victoria** went on a carriage trip to Loch Katrine, then returned by steamboat to Trossachs Pier. She described the carriage ride home from there as 'a long way round Loch Venachar to Invertrossachs: you see the house for three-quarters of an hour before you can get to it. Home at eight. The drive back was lovely, for long after the sun had set the sky remained beautifully pink behind the dark blue hills.'

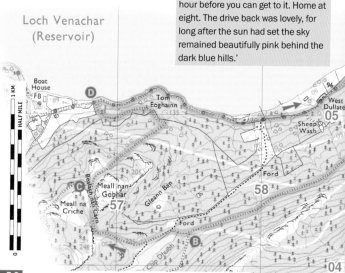

Early morning mist rising from the lochs give the Trossachs that mysterious atmosphere

Left from here, about ½ mile (800m) away is Invertrossachs House. It was built in 1911 to replace a previous house of the same name that had been a favourite with Queen Victoria who was a frequent visitor to the Scottish Highlands throughout the 19th century. In 1869 she travelled extensively throughout the Trossachs from a country house on the south side of Loch Venachar. Prior to her visit the building was known as Drunkie House after the nearby loch. That was however considered to be an unsuitable name for somewhere the Queen would stay and so it was changed to the more romantic Invertrossachs.

Turn right. Continue along this road along the banks of the loch for 1½ miles (2.4km). Just before you reach the two white gate pillars turn right to return to the car park.

A section of the Rob Roy Way from Aberfoyle to Callander joins this walk. This **long-distance footpath** runs from Drymen to Pitlochry for 79 or 92 miles (127 or 148km), depending on which options you choose, following tracks and paths that would have been used by Rob Roy in the 17th and 18th centuries.

15 The Arrochar Alps and Tarbet Loop

This is a gentle walk with a couple of steep sections where the effort of the climb is more than rewarded by the magnificence of the views. On one side are the Arrochar Alps and the length of Loch Long while Loch Lomond and its mighty Ben appear at the other end.

START Arrochar (grid ref: NN 298045)

DISTANCE 4½ miles (7.2km)

TIME 2½ hours

PARKING Lay-by on the A83 opposite Chestnut Cottage, Arrochar

ROUTE FEATURES Mostly woodland and forest roads

From the car park turn right and walk a short distance to pass a red telephone box. Turn right onto

Heading uphill on the Glen Loin footpath

the Glen Loin footpath, pass an interpretation board and head uphill. At a junction Ⓐ turn right onto the path signposted 'Tarbet Station 3.6km'.

Glen Loin runs north from Arrochar and is separated from Loch Lomond by Cruach Tairbeirt. *It is possible to take other, longer walks, along the glen from here but if you do this make sure you take a map with you.* A path leads up the glen for 3½ miles (5.6km) to Coiregrogain and from there a short section of private road goes

PUBLIC TRANSPORT Train from Glasgow

REFRESHMENTS Tarbet tearoom

PUBLIC TOILETS At a car park on the loch side, a little farther along the A83

ORDNANCE SURVEY MAPS Explorer 364 (Loch Lomond North)

to Inveruglas for the lengthy return along the A83. *Alternatively, just past Coiregrogain there is a left turn at a T-junction followed by another a bit farther on, then a further left turn onto a forest road which skirts round the base of A' Chrois to eventually reach Succoth and from there the A83 to Arrochar.*

The path climbs steadily uphill following yellow waymarkers. After a short climb you will reach a viewpoint with a conveniently sited seat where you can pause for a while to get your breath and enjoy the view along Loch Long and across it the impressive summit of

This area was once the territory of **Clan MacFarlane of Arrochar**, almost as notorious for cattle reiving (raiding) as Clan MacGregor . Now it's home to a large variety of birds and wildlife. You might see red deer and roe deer as well as a few red squirrels and the odd fox. There are also buzzards and sparrow hawks with summer visitors including redstarts and pied flycatchers. If you are very lucky you could spot the majestic golden eagle.

The Cobbler with the zigzag access path leading up to it. The summits are composed of intrusive diorites among quartzose mica schists that, according to geologists, is the reason for their unusual shapes.

Loch Long from Arrochar

However local folklore has a more interesting and colourful account. According to legend the south peak is the cobbler, bent over his last with elbows protruding. The north peak is his wife who has spilt some milk which is running down the hillside. This is the Allt a' Bhalachain which is Gaelic for the 'Buttermilk Burn'. Another legend recounts that the body of King Arthur lies asleep under the mountain hence its proper name Ben Arthur. At a mere 109ft (33m) short of munro status, *The Cobbler is another interesting walk but the south peak requires a rock climb and to get onto the north peak you have to pass through the eye of the needle, a small opening which leads to a narrow exposed ledge.* To the right of The Cobbler are the

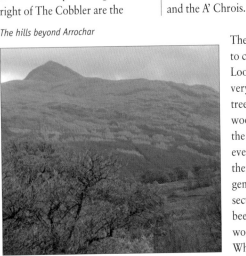

How did Tairbeirt or Tarbet get its name?

peaks of Beinn Narnain and the A' Chrois.

The hills beyond Arrochar

The path continues to climb steadily. Look out for two very old Scots pine trees beside a wooden barrier on the path. The path eventually levels then undulates gently through sections of oak and beech to reach some woodland sculptures. When you reach a

T-junction **B** turn left onto the Cruach Tairbeirt Loop. When the path turns left and heads uphill follow it a short way then ford the burn opposite a red waymarker **C**. Turn right at the other side and follow the red waymarkers back downhill. Follow the path that now runs parallel to the West Highland Railway Line.

This is one of the most scenic railway routes in Britain and runs from Glasgow to Oban and Fort William. The trees will thin and open out to a brilliant view of Loch Lomond and of Ben Lomond rising from the eastern banks. Cross a bridge then head steeply uphill following the course of a burn. At the top of the hill you will come to

another bridge **D** with a picnic table beside it. This is the best spot on the walk for an alfresco lunch. Turn left over the bridge and continue following the red waymarkers. The path keeps climbing until it reaches a T-junction **E**. Turn left and follow the waymarkers back to the spot where you forded the burn **C** and from there retrace your steps back to the start.

The mountains in this part of Scotland are known as the Arrochar Alps. It was here in the 1930s that a new breed of working class climber hitchhiked, took a bus or walked all the way from Glasgow to spend leisure time climbing here, sleeping overnight in caves or under rocks and hedges. Men like **Jock Nimlin, W H Murray and Tom Weir**, who went on to become the legends of Scottish mountaineering, were part of this hardy bunch.

16 *Rest and Be Thankful*

START	Rest and Be Thankful car park (grid ref: NN 229073)
DISTANCE	4½ miles (7.2km)
TIME	3 hours
PARKING	Free car park at start
ROUTE FEATURES	Forest road; old military road

This is probably the most famous stretch of military road in Scotland. It was built in the 18th century as part of the government's plans to subdue the Highlands in the aftermath of the Battle of Culloden. Surfaced to take cars in the early 20th-century, it survived further modernisation when a new road was cut into the hillside above.

🚶 Start from the marker stone in the car park. This was placed here by the military to commemorate the renovation of this section. Veer left from the stone and take the track, which heads uphill, away from the road. At a T-junction with the B828 turn left and walk along it for a short distance to turn left onto a forest road **A** with a signpost for the hill access to Ben Donich.

At the next junction **B** turn left, and continue until the road splits **C**. Take the left fork. The road heads steadily downhill from here along the edge of Glen Croe. Below you to the left is the military road with the modern A83 above it on the far side of the glen.

After his appointment as Commander in Chief of Scotland General Wade built over 250 miles (402km) of roads in the Highlands from 1726 to 1737. The roads successfully allowed the rapid deployment of troops as planned

PUBLIC TRANSPORT Glasgow to Inverary bus
REFRESHMENTS Mobile snack bar in car park
PUBLIC TOILETS None
ORDNANCE SURVEY MAPS Explorer 364 (Loch Lomond North)

On the map:

P &16
Rest and be Thankful
269
244
High Glencroe
07
168
298
A
B
23
C
298
06
24
Quarry (disused)
Old Military Road
A83(T)
Sheep Dip
FB
178
122
P
Laigh Glencroe
98
Croe Water
Glen Croe
E
Tel Ex
D

On the military road

but there was an unexpected side effect – Bonnie Prince Charlie used the roads during the Jacobite Uprising of 1745 to move his own forces and this was one of the reasons he was able to advance so rapidly. Wade, who was 70 years old by then, and a Field Marshall, was appointed Commander in Chief of the army by George II. It was his responsibility to deal with the Uprising but he was not up to

Wade's deputy, Major William Caulfield, who took over in 1740, constructed three times as many miles of road as his predecessor, including this section through Glen Croe. Yet the roads are still called **'Wade Roads'** and it was Wade who was remembered in this little known verse of the National Anthem:

'Lord grant that Marshall Wade
May by thy mighty aid
Victory bring.
May he sedition hush,
And like a torrent rush,
Rebellious Scots to crush.
God save the King!'

the task. He failed to anticipate the movements of the Jacobite forces and as a result they advanced as far as Derby. Wade was replaced by the Duke of Cumberland and died in 1748.

When you reach the bottom of the glen **D** turn left and cross the Croe Water by a bridge. At a T-junction **E** turn left. You are now on the military road. This, in its day, was state of the art and a great improvement on the rough tracks that had existed before. They were built by soldiers, entirely by hand. It was hard, backbreaking toil with each soldier expected to construct about 4ft 6 inches of road every day. To build the roads the turf and the topsoil had to be removed,

Marker stone commemorating the renovation of the road

The military road down Glen Croe from the Rest and Be Thankful

then the surface was excavated until rock or stone was reached. A sledgehammer was then employed to level this with the larger boulders, either levered out or blasted with gunpowder. Once the base was flat 18 inches of gravel was laid on it and compacted using boots and spades. Finally the topsoil was used to form retaining banks at each side of the road and ditches were dug to keep the surface drained of water.

? This road was built in 1748 but when was it repaired?

Go through a gate then cross a stile to continue along the road. Near the end you will find that the road climbs steeply up a series of zigzags returning you to the car park. ●

Although the original military road has a 20th-century surface, if you look closely enough you can still find parts of the road where the modern surface has eroded sufficiently to expose the **original surface** below. You should also be able to see sections where there are still banks of earth created by the removal of topsoil from the road surface and the remains of the ditches the soldiers dug to keep the road drained.

17 Along the Highland Boundary Fault

START Forest Park Visitor Centre (grid ref: NN 518014)
DISTANCE 5¼ miles (8.4km)
TIME 3 hours
PARKING Queen Elizabeth Forest Park Visitor Centre car park (charge)
ROUTE FEATURES Woodland; footpaths; forest roads and old wagon ways

This is an interesting walk, offering the chance to see at first hand the geology that creates the natural division between Lowland and Highland Scotland. This area is also rich in slate and part of the route is along the remnants of the long abandoned wagon ways which were built to transport the stone from the quarries to a railhead.

The walk starts from the car park at the Queen Elizabeth Forest Park Visitor Centre at the David Marshall Lodge. This is ½ mile (800m) from Aberfoyle on the A821.

Leave the car park and cross the A821. Turn right then, almost immediately left **A**, leaving the road to join a narrow path that passes through woodland. Almost straightaway the path forks. Go right and head uphill. This is a rather steep section but should present no difficulties to the average walker. When the path intersects a broader path **B** near the ruins of part of an old wagon way, turn left towards the ruins then immediately right again onto another steep narrow path and continue uphill.

This was part of a wagon way that carried slate from the Aberfoyle quarry via a series of inclined planes to the exchange sidings of the Strathendrick and Aberfoyle Railway below for onward

PUBLIC TRANSPORT Bus from Aberfoyle
REFRESHMENTS David Marshall Lodge, Visitor Centre
PUBLIC TOILETS David Marshall Lodge, Visitor Centre
ORDNANCE SURVEY MAPS Explorer 365 (The Trossachs)

The remains of the wagon way on a hill overlooking the River Forth

transportation to Glasgow. It operated on a similar principle to the one you will encounter later on the walk. It was probably in existence from the opening of the railway in 1882 and closed down in 1947, 12 years before the railway closed. It's overgrown for most of its length and the exchange sidings are now a car park. This is a short but strenuous piece of walk so go slowly. Eventually you will reach the remains of the wagon way where you can pause for a few minutes to enjoy the view back down the hill. Below you to the left is the David Marshall Lodge and farther down the hill the town of Aberfoyle. Looking south you can see the start of the River Forth flowing from Loch Ard and beyond it the ruined church of Kirkton with the distinctive shape of Doon Hill to its left (see Walk 1).

Proceed along the wagon way skirting to the right, round the contours of Craigmore. Keep going through a recently clear felled area ignoring a very old 'path closed' sign to eventually reach a junction with a forest road. The recent felling of the forest means that for the first time in almost 50 years it is possible to see the outline of the surrounding landscape. Continue along the road and enter an area of woodland. When you reach the

Aberfoyle Quarries  keep to the right and follow the road round a hairpin bend and on towards Hill Cottage. At a T-junction with the main road **D** turn right. Walk downhill along the road until you reach a junction with a forest road on your left **E**. Turn into it and proceed to a T-junction **F** then turn right.

At a crossroads **G** keep straight ahead following blue waymarkers. When you reach a conveniently situated picnic table you can pause

This waterfall is passed near the end of the walk

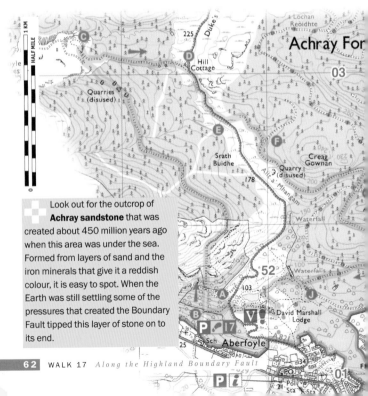

Look out for the outcrop of **Achray sandstone** that was created about 450 million years ago when this area was under the sea. Formed from layers of sand and the iron minerals that give it a reddish colour, it is easy to spot. When the Earth was still settling some of the pressures that created the Boundary Fault tipped this layer of stone on to its end.

for a breather and admire the view or have lunch. A little farther along this road is a sign proclaiming that 'you are standing on the Highland Boundary Fault'. This is a geological line that stretches from Arran to Stonehaven, neatly dividing the country. About 390 million years ago when the Earth was forming, the old rocks of the Highlands were forced up by enormous pressure while the Lowland rocks were pushed down.

Just beyond this at a green waymarker post is a junction **H**. Turn right and head downhill still following blue waymarkers. This steep downhill section was an inclined railway back in the early years of the 19th century. It transported limestone from a quarry above to lime kilns that once stood at the foot of the hill. It consisted of three wooden rails on heavy wooden sleepers. Heavy wooden wagons, attached by wire ropes were used for the transport. The railway worked by sending full wagons down the centre and one outside rail and using their weight to haul

the empty ones back up the centre and other outside rail. A braking mechanism at the top controlled the speed of the wagons while a double section about halfway down allowed the wagons to pass each other. The quarry was exhausted by 1850 and when it was no longer needed the wagon way closed.

> **?** *Which group of rocks are the Highlands around this composed of?*

Look out also for a board marking an outcrop of **Leny grit**. This was created by very high pressure and heat about 550 million years ago. The rock was originally laid down as layers of sand and gravel but the extremes of heat and pressure altered it. In parts it melted and then reformed when it cooled.

When you reach a junction with a forest road **I** turn right then keep ahead at the next junction **J** all the time following blue waymarkers. Turn right at a blue waymark then cross a bridge. Turn right onto a footpath, go past a waterfall, then head uphill. Turn left across a wooden bridge then follow the waymarkers to the David Marshall Lodge where you can enjoy a bowl of the finest soup on offer in all of the National Park. ●

18 *The Glen Ogle Trail*

Although this is the longest walk in the book it is also one of the easiest. With the exception of a short climb at the start it is mostly level. It follows the National Cycle Route along the bed of a former railway on the outward leg and returns on an old military road and some hill tracks.

START From the old railway bridge on the A85 (grid ref: NN 587240)
DISTANCE 6 miles (9.7km)
TIME 3 hours
PARKING On street in Lochearnhead or in the car park ½ mile (800m) away on the edge of the loch
ROUTE FEATURES Old railway line; old military road; hill tracks

One of the distinctive millenium mileposts

This walk starts from the remains of an old railway bridge across the A85 just past its junction with the road to Comrie and Crieff. Just past the bridge there is a lane leading to the Lochearnhead Scout Station. This was formerly Lochearnhead Station in the days of the Callander to Oban Railway.

Go along the lane for a short distance then, at the first bend, veer right onto the Glen Ogle Trail and follow the yellow waymarkers. Almost immediately turn right, go over a stile, through a kissing-gate then take a wet and boggy footpath which heads uphill. The path is well-trodden and easy to follow and eventually you'll encounter the

PUBLIC TRANSPORT Bus from Callander or Killin
REFRESHMENTS Café Lochearnhead
PUBLIC TOILETS Car park
ORDNANCE SURVEY MAPS Explorer 365 (The Trossachs)

odd waymarker confirming that you're still heading in the right direction.

It's a fairly steep climb up the hillside with a height gain of 300ft (91m) in a fifth of a mile so take it easy. After reaching the ruins of a wire fence and the remains of a stile, climb a short, steep section of banking to get onto the former railway line Ⓐ. Look right and left to check for approaching cyclists before turning right and heading along the track bed. This is now part of the National Cycle Network route 7 and the track bed has been resurfaced. Although the trail is climbing from this point up Glen Ogle the gradient is so gentle you'll hardly notice it. Cross a couple of cattle-grids on the route then reach a junction on your left that you should ignore.

Look out for the millennium milepost on the left side of the path just before you cross a viaduct. The views from here along the glen are spectacular. Queen Victoria referred to it as 'Scotland's Khyber Pass'. Below in the glen you can see the line of the military road and above it on the hillside the traffic heading along the modern A85.

> **?** *How many millenium mileposts were erected on the National Cycle Network?*

The Glen Ogle viaduct

Watch out for cyclists

After passing a spectacular waterfall on your left, start to look for your exit from the railway. Cross a bridge and pass another, smaller, waterfall, then veer right up the banking to cross a ladder-stile **B**. Turn right and follow a faint path through the bracken to cross the Ogle Burn on a wooden bridge, then take the waymarked path to the left. This follows the course of the burn. This is a rather wet and boggy section. Follow it to cross an old stone bridge which probably dates back to the building of the military road. Continue to cross another bridge and by then you should be able to make out the outline of the military road.

At times, particularly during wet weather the surface resembles a riverbed rather than an old road but continue to follow the line and you'll find some sections where the original layout of the military road can be seen and examined. Now your view is reversed and you can see the line of the railway running along the side of the glen to your right. The viaduct will come into view so you can appreciate how spectacular it is.

Again the road will become indistinct but keep heading in the same direction and an occasional solitary waymarker will confirm that you're on the right track. You are passing an area where a massive landslide blocked the glen in August 2004 after weeks of exceptionally heavy rain. Cross two small wooden bridges then head left up towards the road, where the path ends at a ladder-stile **C**. Cross this, and then after crossing the A85, continue on a waymarked path on the other side.

Cross another stile then veer right to go through a gate and immediately ford a burn. The route continues from here on a well-waymarked path. You have several burns to ford, none of them a problem, then cross the Ogle on a wooden footbridge **D**. Turn left to follow a path that leads to a

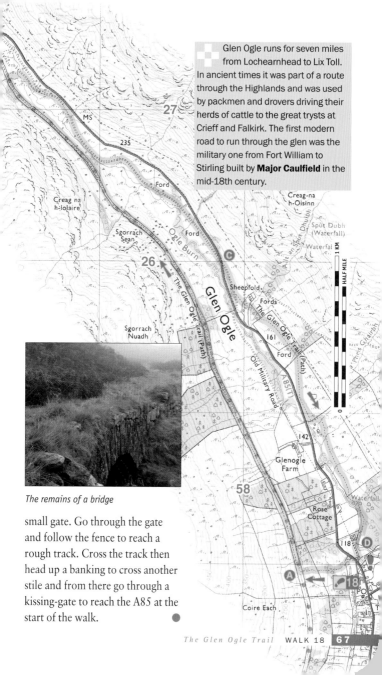

Glen Ogle runs for seven miles from Lochearnhead to Lix Toll. In ancient times it was part of a route through the Highlands and was used by packmen and drovers driving their herds of cattle to the great trysts at Crieff and Falkirk. The first modern road to run through the glen was the military one from Fort William to Stirling built by **Major Caulfield** in the mid-18th century.

The remains of a bridge

small gate. Go through the gate and follow the fence to reach a rough track. Cross the track then head up a banking to cross another stile and from there go through a kissing-gate to reach the A85 at the start of the walk.

19 Glen Croe and the Cats Craig Loop

START Ardgartan Tourist Information Office (grid ref: NN 269037)
DISTANCE 5¼ miles (8.4km)
TIME 3 hours
PARKING Free at Ardgartan Tourist Information Office
ROUTE FEATURES Forest roads; footpath; woodland

This is an easy walk along forest roads and a quiet lane. It's waymarked as a cycle route but there's no warning of the short, downhill section of path linking two sections of forest road. It's steep and has steps – ideal and easy for the walker, however all but the most advanced bikers would have to get off and carry their cycles.

The walk starts from a small car park near the Ardgartan Tourist Information Office, just off the A83 near the foot of Glen Croe. Pass the tourist office and cross the Croe Water by a bridge to reach the small walkers' car park. Glen Croe marks the northern boundary of an area known as the Cowal Peninsula. From here, head uphill on a forest road marked 'Cats Craig Loop North'. *As this is also a favorite cycle route you should keep your eyes and ears open for cyclists approaching downhill.* The road climbs gently and part way up an area of recent felling opens onto splendid views up Glen Croe and across it to The Cobbler.

Back in the days before the military road was built along Glen Croe it was still a major communications artery and used by travellers, peddlers and cattle drovers. From the 17th to 19th centuries droving accounted for a large part of the Highland economy. Owing to the lack of winter fodder, surplus cattle had to be driven to the great cattle markets, or 'trysts', at Crieff and Falkirk for sale and onward transmission to destinations as far away as England. With no roads in

PUBLIC TRANSPORT Bus from Glasgow to Inverary
REFRESHMENTS Tarbet tearoom 4 miles
PUBLIC TOILETS Nearest are in Arrochar 2½ miles
ORDNANCE SURVEY MAPS Explorer 364 (Loch Lomond North)

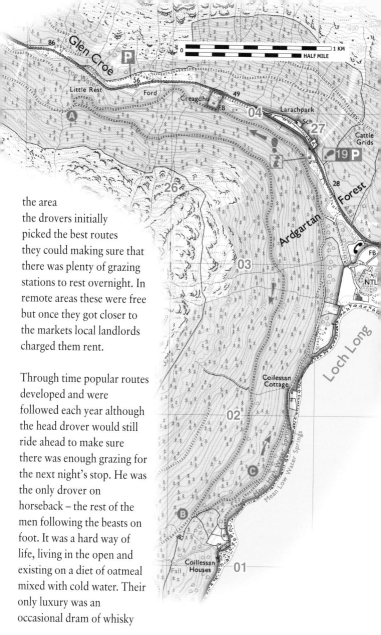

the area
the drovers initially
picked the best routes
they could making sure that
there was plenty of grazing
stations to rest overnight. In
remote areas these were free
but once they got closer to
the markets local landlords
charged them rent.

Through time popular routes
developed and were
followed each year although
the head drover would still
ride ahead to make sure
there was enough grazing for
the next night's stop. He was
the only drover on
horseback – the rest of the
men following the beasts on
foot. It was a hard way of
life, living in the open and
existing on a diet of oatmeal
mixed with cold water. Their
only luxury was an
occasional dram of whisky

The most spectacular of the waterfalls on the Cats Craig Loop

from the ram's horn they carried it in. Occasionally they might get some ewe's milk cheese and a bannock (round, flat loaf) when they passed a settlement, and when supplies started to run low they would supplement their rations by bleeding the cattle and mixing the blood with oatmeal to make black puddings. Large numbers of cattle from the islands and the west came through Inverary, past the head of Loch Fyne and carried on down from there towards Glen Croe and on to Loch Long. From there they would continue to Balloch before cutting inland to cross to Stirling and Falkirk.

After walking uphill for just over a

The **end of cattle droving** started in the mid-19th century when the Industrial Revolution began creating new ways of communication. Steamships proved to be a more profitable way to transport cattle from the islands, and when the railways arrived it was the end of the trail. By the 20th century the Falkirk Tryst was all but gone and droving on a large scale was consigned to history.

mile turn left at a T-junction Ⓐ and continue along another forest road. Shortly after the junction there's another viewpoint with a picnic table where you can rest and have a snack, although there's another table farther round the route that makes a better lunch stop. Thereafter continue following this road and the cycle waymarks. The road undulates a bit but overall you are continuing to gain altitude. At the end of this section of forest road there is a clearing and beyond it the route continues on a footpath. Shortly it starts a rather steep climb to reach a small wooden bridge. From here you will have the best view of the most spectacular of the waterfalls passed on this walk.

> **?** *You can see a mountain called The Cobbler from the viewpoints on this walk but what is its real name?*

There is a plaque near the bridge which was built by the Prince's Trust and opened by Prince Charles in 1982 although he probably came up in a Land-Rover and only walked the last few yards. Keep climbing uphill after the bridge on a narrow, rocky path then descend on an even rougher section. *You need to take care on the descent particularly if the ground is wet* and although there is nothing dangerous here for walkers just imagine what it would be like to hurtle down on a bike! Once off the path there is a level section with a picnic table. From here the views open out and you can see up Loch Long to Arrochar with the top of Cruach Tairbeirt behind it. To your right, across the loch are Ben Reoch and Tullich Hill while to the left you can see all three summits of The Cobbler and to the right of that the summit of Ben Narnain with its 'Spearhead' is also visible. On a good day this is the best spot for a lunch stop.

From here it's a reasonable walk along a forest road then downhill to reach a barrier at a T-junction **B** where you join the surfaced lane. Turn left here and continue downhill to reach the junction **C** leading to Coilessan and the loch side. Keep left at the junction and continue along this road for just over one mile (1.6km) to return to the car park. On the way you will pass the entrance to Ardgartan caravan park.

●

The steep climb to the waterfall

20 *Loch Drunkie*

START Forestry Commission car park off the Duke's Pass Road (grid ref: NN 519037)

DISTANCE 5½ miles (8.8km)

TIME 3 hours

PARKING Free at Forestry Commission car park

ROUTE FEATURES Forest roads; footpath; road; woodland; loch

Most of this exceedingly pleasant walk is on forest road with just a short section at the end on some rough footpaths and a section along the A821. Following the route of a forest drive and part of the National Cycle Trail it is particularly good for children and has a splendid play area mid-way.

👟 Leave the car park and keep left to follow the Forest Drive signs and pass the toll barrier. Pass Lochan Reoidhte on your right, then reach a crossroads and turn left onto the National Cycle Trail, route 7 **A**. Continue on the forest road as it heads round a hairpin bend ignoring all other junctions.

You are now in a section of the forest that has reached the end of its first commercial cycle. The mature trees have been harvested and all that is left are a few dead trees and others where the wind has snapped the stems. They have not been felled but have been left in place to provide perches for the birds of prey that live in the forest. From these vantage points they can spy out their next meal before rising into the air and swooping on their unsuspecting victim.

The dead wood that remains is also an ideal habitat for insects that lay their eggs there, thus providing a constant supply of food for the woodpeckers and other birds of the

PUBLIC TRANSPORT Bus from Aberfoyle

REFRESHMENTS Queen Elizabeth Forest Park Visitor Centre

PUBLIC TOILETS At car park halfway round walk

ORDNANCE SURVEY MAPS Explorer 365 (The Trossachs)

forest. Other areas have been left alone to ensure that the seed-eating birds and squirrels have enough food for their survival. If the woods were stripped bare they could not live here.

To prepare the harvested area for the planting of new seedlings a special type of tractor, called a 'scarifier', has been used. It creates bare patches amongst the tangle of dead branches and it's these spots that will receive the new seedlings. In time they will grow into mature trees, be harvested and the cycle will start all over again. The seedlings that are to be planted now are different from before. Gone are the days of blanket planting with regimented rows of Sitka spruce marching along the hillsides. Foresters now plan a varied scheme, which includes

Scots' pines, larch and Norway spruce as well as deciduous trees like alder, oak, willow, birch, hawthorn and rowan. Although it will take many years before the results of this scheme can be seen, it will help to ensure the survival of wildlife and provide a valuable legacy for future generations.

When you reach a junction to the left ignore it and keep on the main road. You will arrive at a group of picnic tables, which provide one of the best spots to lunch in the park **B**. To your right is a breathtaking view over Loch Drunkie. When the forest around this area is due for harvest and replanting the foresters intend to leave some of the crags and rocky outcrops visible so that visitors can get an idea of the geological composition. Likewise some old buildings that were cleared years ago and swallowed by the forest will be uncovered and left on view.

> According to the label on bottles of a ten-year-old malt whisky called **Loch Drunkie**, the loch was named after the days when illicit **whisky** was distilled on its shores. When the moonshiners heard that the excise man was approaching they hid their barrels in the loch. Unfortunately some of them leaked into the water and that is how the loch got its name.

Continue from the picnic table and turn right at the next junction. Follow the road as it loops round Loch Drunkie then heads uphill to reach a car park. Here you will find toilets, more picnic tables and a children's playground. Continue along the road from the car park ignoring the left turn **C** then reach a junction **D** and turn left. You are still on the cycle route so follow the markers to reach Black Water Marshes. This is a raised bog and a Site of Special Scientific Interest (SSSI). Here you can see willow and birch trees and patches of bog myrtle. Greylag geese, widgeon, teal and goosanders all make themselves at home here and

This short section of footpath can be boggy in wet weather

Most of this walk is on pleasant forest roads and tracks

special efforts are being made to encourage barn owls to take up residence. See if you can spot any of the nesting boxes that have been installed for them. Many small creatures grub around here foraging for food while above them birds of prey hover ready to dine on them. Across the marsh you can see the entrance to Glen Finglas and the conical peak of Ben A'an to its left.

> **?** *Can you name the trees around the clearing at the children's play area?*

Continue along the road from here to reach a junction **E**. Turn left and head uphill on a forest road. At the next junction **F** turn right and continue for ½ mile (800m) to reach another junction **G**. Keeping in the same direction cut across the forest road and take a faint path uphill through the trees. Do not worry if you cannot see this from the road, just walk straight ahead and it will appear. This gets very boggy, particularly after spells of prolonged wet weather but keep on it all the way up to cross a rough track. Eventually the path will clear the trees to reach open hillside. From here continue across some rough ground then exit onto the main road **H**. Turn left and follow the road uphill ¾ mile (1.2km) to the car park.

●

Further Information

Safety on the Hills

The hills, mountains and moorlands of Britain, though of modest height compared with those in many other countries, need to be treated with respect. Friendly and inviting in good weather, they can quickly be transformed into wet, misty, windswept and potentially dangerous areas of wilderness in bad weather. Even on an outwardly fine and settled summer day, conditions can rapidly deteriorate. In winter, of course, the weather can be even more erratic and the hours of daylight are much shorter.

Look out for interesting fungi

Therefore it is advisable to always take both warm and waterproof clothing, sufficient nourishing food, a hot drink, first-aid kit, torch and whistle. Wear suitable footwear, such as strong walking boots or shoes that give a good grip over rocky terrain and on slippery slopes. Try to obtain a local weather forecast and bear it in mind before you start. Do not be afraid to abandon your proposed route and return to your starting point in the event of a sudden and unexpected deterioration in the weather. Do not go alone. Allow enough time to finish the walk well before nightfall.

Most of the walks described in this book do not venture into remote wilderness areas and will be safe to do, given due care and respect, at any time of year in all but the most unreasonable weather. Indeed, a crisp, fine winter day often provides perfect walking conditions, with firm ground underfoot and a clarity that is not possible to achieve in the other seasons of the year. A few walks, however, are suitable only for reasonably fit and experienced hill walkers able to use a compass and should definitely not be tackled

This seat at Creag an Tuirc (Walk 2) has one of the finest views in the Highlands

by anyone else during the winter months or in bad weather, especially high winds and mist. These are indicated in the general description that precedes each of the walks.

Follow the Country Code

- Enjoy the countryside and respect its life and work
- Guard against all risk of fire
- Take your litter home
- Fasten all gates
- Help to keep all water clean
- Keep your dogs under control
- Protect wildlife, plants and trees
- Keep to public paths across farmland
- Take special care on country roads
- Leave livestock, crops and machinery alone
- Make no unnecessary noise
- Use gates and stiles to cross fences, hedges and walls

(The Countryside Agency)

Useful Organisations

The Camping and Caravanning Club
Greenfields House,
Westwood Way, Coventry
CV4 8JH
Tel. 024 7669 4995
www.campingandcaravanningclub.co.uk

Historic Scotland
Longmore House,
Salisbury Place, Edinburgh
EH9 1SH
Tel. 0131 6688600
www.historic-scotland.gov.uk

The National Park Gateway Centre
Loch Lomond Shores, Balloch
Tel. 0845 345 4978
www.lochlomond-trossachs.org

National Park Centres

Balmaha
Tel. 013608 70470
Luss
Tel. 01301 702785

National Trust for Scotland
Wemyss House,
28 Charlotte Square,
Edinburgh
EH2 4ET
Tel. 0131 2439300
www.nts.org.uk

Ordnance Survey
Romsey Road,
Maybush,
Southampton
SO16 4GU
Tel. 08456 050505 (Lo-call)
www.ordnancesurvey.co.uk

Loch Katrine

Ramblers' Association Scotland
Kingfisher House,
Auld Mart Business Park,
Milnathort,
Kinross
KY13 9DA
Tel. 01577 861222
www.ramblers.org.uk/scotland

RSPB Scotland
Dunedin House,
25 Ravelston Terrace,
Edinburgh
EH4 3TP
Tel. 0131 3116500
www.rspb.org.uk/scotland

Scottish Natural Heritage
12 Hope Terrace,
Edinburgh
EH9 2AS
Tel. 0131 4474784
www.snh.org.uk

Scottish Youth Hostels Association
7 Glebe Crescent,
Stirling
FK8 2JA
Tel. 01786 891400
www.syha.org.uk

Tourist Information Centres
Scottish Tourist Board
Visit Scotland National
Information Centre
Tel. 0845 2255121
www.visitscotland.com

Local Tourist Information Centres
Aberfoyle
Open April – October
November – March
(weekends only)
Tel. 0870 7200 604

Ardgartan
Open April – October
Tel. 0870 7200 606

Balloch
Open April – October
Tel. 01389 753533

Callander
Open March – December
January – February
(weekends only)
Tel. 0870 7200 628

Tarbet
Open April – October
Tel. 0870 7200 623

Public Transport
Traveline Scotland
29 Drumsheugh Gardens,
Edinburgh
EH3 7RN
www.travelinescotland.com

Ordnance Survey Maps
Explorers
Explorer 347 Loch Lomond South
Explorer 364 Loch Lomond North
Explorer 365 The Trossachs

Answers to Questions

Walk 1: Mort safes, which were used to stop body snatchers from getting into the coffins.

Walk 2: 'MacGregor Despite Them'.

Walk 3: Rough water.

Walk 4: Sir Walter Scott.

Walk 5: This mark is used on Scottish long-distance footpaths. In this case it is the West Highland Way that runs from Milngavie to Fort William.

Walk 6: On the opposite side of the stone wall from the path.

Walk 7: It means Beacon Hill.

Walk 8: An acorn.

Walk 9: It means the big fort.

Walk 10: Ben Lomond.

Walk 11: It comes from the Gaelic 'tuirc' meaning 'boar'.

Walk 12: The red squirrel

Walk 13: *SS Sir Walter Scott*.

Walk 14: Fossils.

Walk 15: It comes from a Viking word meaning portage. King Hakon and his men dragged their longboats from Loch Long, over the narrow strip of land between there and Loch Lomond.

Walk 16: According to the stone in the car park erected by the soldiers who repaired this section, it was 1768.

Walk 17: The Dalradian group.

Walk 18: One thousand.

Walk 19: Ben Arthur.

Walk 20: Birch, Norway spruce, Douglas fir, Scots pine, oak and larch.

Mountain scenery in Glen Finglas (Walk 11)